PATCHOGUE

This is probably the earliest image of Patchogue. It was taken in 1868 looking southwest from the roof of Roe's Eagle Hotel on East Main Street. The intersection of Church Street and South Ocean Avenue can be seen just to the right of the large barn on the left. (Courtesy of the Greater Patchogue Historical Society.)

PAST & PRESENT

PATCHOGUE

Steven M. Lucas

This volume is dedicated to my wife, Rosemary, whose encouragement and assistance proved to be invaluable. Her efforts as typist and proofreader were instrumental in making the idea become a reality. In addition to the love of my life, she is also my best friend.

Published by Arcadia Publishing
Charleston, South Carolina

For all general information, please contact Arcadia Publishing:
Telephone 843-853-2070
Fax 843-853-0044
E-mail sales@arcadiapublishing.com
For customer service and orders:
Toll-Free 1-888-313-2665

Visit us on the Internet at www.arcadiapublishing.com

ON THE FRONT COVER: These photographs were taken looking west at the intersection of Main Street with North and South Ocean Avenues. The c. 1910 image of Patchogue's famous Four Corners shows Swezey and Newins Department Store on the northwest corner. With the bunting on many of the buildings and a large crowd gathered, it appears that a parade is about to start or has just ended. Today's photograph shows the New Village Apartments complex dominating the former Swezey's site. (Courtesy of the Greater Patchogue Historical Society.)

ON THE BACK COVER: This 1892 photograph shows the "Rocket," an experimental electric monorail train car, on its way to East Patchogue for test runs on a one-and-a-half-mile track near Dunton Avenue. Passing through Patchogue's famous Four Corners, it had been pulled by oxen from Brooklyn because the Long Island Railroad viewed it as competition and refused to transport it on a flatbed railroad car. (Courtesy of the Greater Patchogue Historical Society.)

CONTENTS

ACKNOWLEDGMENTS

During the US bicentennial year of 1976, many local events and celebrations sparked a greater interest in preserving history. Oral histories of Patchogue were becoming more common during everyday conversations among Patchogue residents.

The Greater Patchogue Historical Society was founded in 1982 by a small group of like-minded individuals who simply wanted to get together and talk about the "good old days of Patchogue." Occasionally, a guest speaker would be invited to present a program related to a specific topic of local history. Two Patchogue village historians, Francis "Bucko" Logan and Anne King Swezey, were among the early members of the organization. Anne was also dedicated to the preservation of the 1858 Swan River Schoolhouse in East Patchogue, which had been operated as a local museum by the Town of Brookhaven. Interpretations and tours of the schoolhouse were given to school groups by Anne and Marjorie Roe, another early member. These tours continue to this day by society volunteers.

Membership in the Greater Patchogue Historical Society steadily grew, leading to members looking for a location to donate their artifacts and memorabilia related to Patchogue history. Some items were stored in the schoolhouse, some in the old Brookhaven Town Hall on South Ocean Avenue, and some in the Patchogue Village Hall. The ever-increasing size of the collection of artifacts led to the eventual opening of the historical society's museum in the restored Carnegie Library building.

Starting in 1997, current Patchogue village historian Hans Henke has written four books detailing the many facets of Patchogue history: Images of America: *Patchogue*; Images of America: *Patchogue, Volume II*; *Patchogue: The Early Years*; and *Patchogue in the Twentieth Century*. It is with a deep sense of appreciation and gratitude that the author wishes to thank Hans Henke for doing the research for his books that allowed for the completion of this volume.

The past images in this publication are from the archives of the Greater Patchogue Historical Society, which has graciously allowed the author to access and use them. The present images were taken by the author.

INTRODUCTION

The history and development of the village of Patchogue, and to some extent the surrounding unincorporated area, can be compared to the so-called nine lives of a cat. The Native Americans who first inhabited the area were hunter-gatherers, but they were not members of a Patchogue tribe, as some sources indicate. That designation never existed. The name "Patchogue" is derived from an indigenous word, *pauchaug*, which roughly translates to "where three streams meet." By 1812, a small settlement of 75 non-native residents had developed.

During the past 200 years, the Patchogue community has evolved and reinvented itself many times. Originally a farming and agricultural area, it gradually became more dependent on commercial fishing, shellfish harvesting, and boatbuilding. Several mills designed for various purposes were built throughout the 19th century along the three streams. Many boatyards were built along the Patchogue River; by 1892, there were 12 of them.

With the arrival of the railroad in 1869, a significant resort industry developed, along with many hotels and several large estates. This period of prosperity for the hotel industry lasted from the 1880s into the 1920s. At one time, there were over 35 establishments catering to travelers and vacationers in the Patchogue area. It was "the Hamptons" before the Hamptons.

Within a relatively short time, many of the larger tracts of land were subdivided into residential building lots, and Patchogue became a bedroom community. This necessitated the arrival of many small- and medium-sized retail establishments, and Patchogue became a major shopping area for most of Suffolk County. With the advent of shopping malls and big-box stores, Patchogue went into a period of economic decline as more and more mom-and-pop stores closed and were not replaced.

This brings us to the current reinvention that has taken place over the past 20 years. Careful higher-density residential construction, combined with a repurposed retail, restaurant, bar, and cultural arts environment, has allowed Patchogue to become one of the most vibrant places in the country.

An employee at the Blue Point Brewery recently inquired about a rumor that parachutes were once manufactured in her building during World War II. A visitor to the Greater Patchogue Historical Society's museum asked, "Where was Swezey's located?" Still another question came from a person in California, who wondered if his grandparents' home on Bay Avenue still stood. These are the types of questions I hope to answer in this book along with the story of Patchogue's many incarnations.

CHAPTER 1

MAIN STREET

The Anchorage Inn was a popular restaurant operated by Will Graham from about 1900 through the 1920s. Although labeled as Patchogue, it was actually located on the north side of Montauk Highway (Main Street) in Blue Point, approximately 1,000 yards west of Patchogue. The inn has not survived, but the sphinx was moved and can still be seen at Fontana Concrete Products in Bayport, New York.

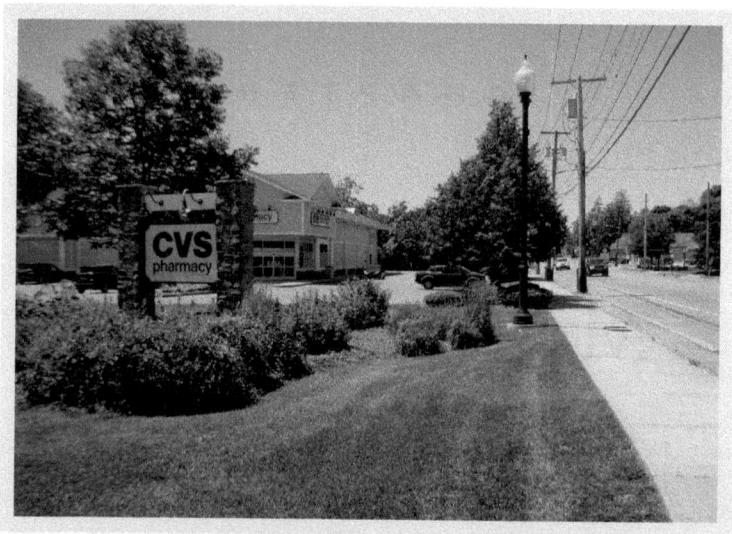

On the southwest corner of Main Street and South Prospect Avenue, the residence of Ernest E. Brown also served as his photography business and studio. Brown was among several commercial photographers working in Patchogue about 1910, the date of this early image. Several of the postcards in this book can be attributed to him. The CVS is one of several pharmacies built in Patchogue where historic buildings once stood.

Lace Mill. Patchogue, N. Y.

The Patchogue Lace Mill, as it was commonly known, had its origin in the 1850s as the Union Twine Mills, on the north side of West Main Street at the south end of Patchogue Lake. This c. 1920 view was taken looking east and shows only about 10 percent of the huge complex. Also referred to as "Patchogue College," the mill employed about 200 people in the 1890s.

Lace Mills, Patchogue, L. I.

M17114

This view, from about the same time as the previous photograph, is looking west and gives more of an indication of how large the site was. Continuous expansion through the early 1920s allowed the mill to increase its workforce to approximately 600. Business declined through the 1930s and 1940s until it closed in 1954. After the closing, Island Industrial Park bought the site, refurbished many of the buildings, and leased them to various businesses. Several major fires starting in the 1970s led to new construction for Swezey's department store (2000), Briarcliffe College (2004), the YMCA, and finally, Blue Point Brewery.

Situated at 24 West Main Street, the Central Hotel was one of many locations in Patchogue where rooms could be rented by the day, week, or season. Operated by Clay Losee in the 1880s and later by D.J. Thurber and his son, the daily rate was $2 at the time of this c. 1905 photograph. The hotel had space for up to 100 patrons. The building is still there but contains offices and stores, most notably Gino's Pizza.

Central Hotel, Patchogue, L. I.

The Citizens Trust Company Bank building, at 47 West Main Street, opened to the public in 1925, about when this photograph was taken. It began operations in 1903, merged with the Patchogue Bank and Trust Company in 1933, and subsequently shortened its name to the Patchogue Bank. Through mergers and acquisitions, it later became Island State Bank, Norstar Bank, and Bank of America.

Masonic Temple, PATCHOGUE, N. Y.

2020

This is an early rendering of the Masonic lodge building prior to its construction about 1905. It was on the north side of West Main Street at number 55. It was built at a cost of $15,000 by Edwin Bailey and sold to the Masons in 1906. The grocery store of Mathieu, Reid, and Shand was on the ground floor. During the 1940s and 1950s, a public restroom with attendant occupied part of the ground floor also. The Island State Bank acquired the site for its drive-up windows after fire destroyed the lodge in 1974.

The Aldrich Electric Store was at 14 East Main Street, slightly east of the Four Corners, in the Mills Building. This 1927 photograph has William Aldrich proudly standing in front of his shop along with his delivery truck, a Ford Model T. An electrical contractor, Aldrich also sold electric supplies including radios, ranges, and appliances. A 1956 fire claimed the Mills Building, but small retail stores still operate at the site.

This image from about 1919 could have been taken from in front of Aldrich's store and shows Roe's Hotel on the north side of Main Street. The original section on the right with the cupola was built in 1851. The large extension to the left was added in 1892, bringing overnight capacity to 200 guests. A major fire in 1934 destroyed most of the hotel, with the site subsequently being gradually developed into small retail shops.

643

TEL, PATCHOGUE, LONG ISLAND, N. Y.

Construction began for the Congregational church in 1892, with the dedication taking place the following year. The cost was $46,815. Established in 1793, the Congregational community at one time shared an 1820 building with the Methodists, Presbyterians, and Baptists on the northeast corner of Waverly Avenue and West Main Street. Listed in the National Register of Historic Places in 1993, it has changed little over the years since the early photograph from 1907.

Congregational Church, Patchogue, L. I.

THE PATCHOGUE HOTEL,
PATCHOGUE, LONG ISLAND, N. Y.

Constructed in 1925–1926 as the Elks Hotel and Clubhouse after their much smaller building was moved to West Main Street to become an apartment house, this building was utilized by the Elks until 1936. It stood vacant until 1941, when it was repurposed as the Patchogue Hotel. Many local events such as weddings, graduations, and business meetings were held in the large third-floor hall. Demolished in 1969, it is now the site of the Tiffany apartments at Maple Avenue and East Main Street.

The Patchogue Post Office was constructed in 1932–1933 and was the first federal building in Suffolk County. It was designed by the noted architect John V. Van Pelt, who was a resident of Patchogue. Prior post offices were located in office buildings or in a local business with the business owner acting as the appointed postmaster. Built in the Art Deco/Classical Revival style and listed in the National Register of Historic Places in 1989, it has not changed much in 87 years.

The residence of Judge Walter H. Jaycox on the north side of East Main Street at number 239 was one of a large number of stately mansions that once occupied both sides of the road. Jaycox became a lawyer in 1889 and later served as Suffolk County district attorney, New York Supreme Court judge, and appellate division judge. The home was built in approximately 1905 and served as the residence for Judge Jaycox and his wife, Inez, until his death in 1927.

DENCE OF JUDGE W. H. JAYCOX, MAIN ST., PATCHOGUE, N.Y.

This image shows the second Xeller's Restaurant, on the south side of East Main Street at the foot of Medford Avenue (Route 112). The first Xeller's was on the northwest corner of East Main Street and Maple Avenue, opposite the Elks lodge, where William Xeller was also the manager in 1926. Today the site is occupied by Avenue Sound at 260 and Advance Auto Parts at 252.

Xeller's Restaurant & Grill opposite Medford Ave. Beacon Light, E. Main St., Patchogue

Barrie Brothers, selling Oldsmobiles and Cadillacs, had been at this location of 318 East Main Street since the 1930s. The 1956 photograph shows the new 1957 models. In the 1940s, this area also included a Lincoln-Mercury dealer at 320 and a Packard showroom at 322. Today's photograph shows very little change to the building except for the subdivision into L.I. Bicycles and Main Street Fireplace.

THE OLD OAK HOTEL, PATCHOGUE, N. Y.

The Old Oak Hotel was on the north side of East Main Street at 369. It had been a private residence until 1895, when it was purchased by George A. Link, who converted it to a hotel and restaurant. Prior to it being destroyed by fire in 1950, the Link family had the reputation of serving only the finest food. The menu at today's Dunkin Donuts is quite different.

NORTH AND SOUTH
OCEAN AVENUES

This photograph was probably taken from the top of the Patchogue Fire Department tower about 1880 looking north on Pine Street, later renamed North Ocean Avenue. The Congregational church, built in 1855, can be seen on the corner of Lake Street.

After the new church was built on East Main Street, the building was sold, enlarged, and converted to the Lyceum Theatre. Oak Street can be seen at lower right.

This 1918 view looking north on North Ocean Avenue shows the trolley returning from the Holtsville station of the Long Island Railroad. Although it was more commonly called the Patchogue Trolley, it was actually a storage battery streetcar, one of four operated by the Suffolk Traction Company between Sayville, Bayport, Blue Point, Patchogue, and Holtsville. Swezey and Newins department store is on the left, with McBride's Drug Store on the right. The drugstore building still stands, with O'Neill's Sales Exchange as the tenant. Arooga's restaurant is now on the opposite corner.

The Holtsville Trolley, Patchogue, L. I.

Ocean Av., Patchogue, L. I.

Looking north on North Ocean Avenue from Cedar Grove Street in this c. 1907 view, one can see two of the large residences that were among several that lined both sides of the road. In today's photograph, the corner house is still there, although no longer on the corner. The property has been divided into two lots, with a newer home now closer to Cedar Grove Street.

Ocean Ave., South, from Main St.
Patchogue, L.I.

This c. 1920 photograph was taken looking south on South Ocean Avenue from Main Street. The Mills Building is on the left with several retail shops on the ground level, including dentists Overton and Robbins and the F.W. Woolworth store. On the right are several individual buildings containing Bailey's Hardware and Brandau's Butcher Shop, among others. In today's view, the look and feel are similar, but the only real constant is the steeple of the Patchogue United Methodist Church in the distance.

This view shows approximately the same area as the previous page, only with the camera facing north and the date about 10 years earlier. The three distinct sections of the very large Mills Building, starting at the corner and going south, are readily apparent. Swezey and Newins department store is in the center of the Four Corners intersection. Today's view actually has more of an openness to it, and many of the small retail shops are now restaurants. New Village Apartments has replaced Swezey and Newins.

So. Ocean Avenue and Main Street,
Patchogue, L. I.

The Union Savings Bank is the dominant building in this c. 1913 view of the northwest corner of Church Street and South Ocean Avenue. It had only recently been constructed in 1911, after the bank moved from its previous location in the Tower Building, which had Swezey and Newins on the ground floor. Built in the Georgian style of architecture and covered in white Vermont marble, it looks much the same today as it did then. Now owned by the Industrial Coverage Corporation, it was listed in the National Register of Historic Places in 2010.

OCEAN AVENUE, SHOWING UNION SAVINGS BANK, PATCHOGUE, L. I.

CHOGUE, N. Y.   H. S. Conklin's

The stationery store of Howard S. Conklin was at 29 South Ocean Avenue on the east side of the road in the Arcade Building. In addition to books and stationery, Conklin sold sporting goods, toys, legal forms, Patchogue souvenirs, and many other items. He was also an authorized dealer for Kodak cameras and a professional photographer. Many of his postcards provide a valuable historic archive. Today's image shows the same address with a newer building.

Original STAR THEATRE, PATCHOGUE, L. I.

The original Star Palace theater was at approximately 75–77 South Ocean Avenue on the east side of the road. This photograph from about 1907 advertises the various forms of entertainment that were popular at the time. A new Star Palace was built on West Main Street in 1910. The original theater was begun by George Holmes, a butcher by trade. Ironically, the site was later occupied by Smith's Meat Market. Today's photograph shows that music can still be heard there.

This c. 1912 photograph shows another view of South Ocean Avenue looking north, this time from south of Terry Street. The Patchogue United Methodist Church on the left has not changed at all since its construction in 1889. It was listed in the National Register of Historic Places in 1984 and includes several Tiffany windows. The corner of Terry Street is on the right.

OCEAN AVENUE SHOWING M. E. CHURCH, PATCHOGUE, L. I.

The Unique Theatre was one of several entertainment venues in Patchogue when this photograph was taken around 1910. Owned by Nat Goldstein, the building also housed a ladies' parlor offering shampoos, scalp treatments, facial massages, and manicures. Located just north of Gerard Street, the Unique moved several buildings north on South Ocean Avenue and later became the Rialto Theatre. Part of a copper beech tree is visible on the left, which gave its name to the apartments in today's photograph.

TOWN HALL, PATCHOGUE, LONG ISLAND, N.Y.

The Brookhaven Town Hall was on the east side of South Ocean Avenue just south of the railroad tracks at number 199. It served as the home of Brookhaven town government from about the time of this photograph in the mid-1920s until 1986, when most of the town functions moved to Medford. Although vacant for many years, the building was recently modernized and repurposed by Northwell Health.

Patchogue Post, American Legion, Patchogue, L. I.

The American Legion Post No. 269 was chartered on August 15, 1919. The building is at 215 South Ocean Avenue at the corner of Baker Street and dates to 1924, about the time of this photograph. The current image shows that the building has remained mostly unchanged. The Patchogue Village Hall became a neighbor in 1935. The original Civil War veterans' statue was recently restored.

The Laurel House Hotel stood on the northwest corner of Laurel Street and South Ocean Avenue. Constructed in the early 1880s by John S. Silsbe Sr., it was originally open only during the summer season. It was subsequently owned by Gelston Roe. The past photograph dates from about 1912. The building was razed many years ago, and the property is now the site of several private residences.

THE LAUREL HOUSE, PATCHOGUE, L. I.

The White House Hotel stood at 522 South Ocean Avenue and was one of the smaller establishments that offered accommodations during the summer season. It was operated by A. Wissler at the time of this 1942 photograph. Only a short walk from the Great South Bay, it offered the same cooling breezes at a more modest rate than most of the other places. After falling into disrepair for many years, it was demolished for the Bay Village Condominiums in 2006.

THE WHITE HOUSE
522 S. Ocean Ave.   Patchogue,
A. Wissler, Prop.   Tel. 105

SMITHPORT HOTEL, PATCHOGUE, N. Y.

The Smithport Hotel, like its neighbor the White House, was built as a seasonal boardinghouse. Constructed about 1880 by Capt. Samuel Smith, it became a year-round hotel during ownership by his daughter Ruth Newey Smith in 1898. Throughout its glory days, it could accommodate up to 40 guests, but it suffered a steady decline until finally being condemned and demolished in 2006 as part of the Bay Village project.

High School, Patchogue, N.Y.

A 10 630

The high school, or academy as it was sometimes called, was on the southeast corner of South Ocean Avenue and Academy Street. The school was constructed in 1871; this 1908 image was probably a rendering used to show the proposed addition in the rear. The Civil War veterans' statue is the same one that was later relocated to the American Legion property. The current site, although not a school, is still a popular stop for students looking for a snack on their way to or from the replacement school two blocks away.

This 1906 image of the Patchogue United Methodist Church bears witness to the extreme changes that can take place in a community in slightly more than four generations. The previously mentioned Unique Theatre, Rialto Theatre, and Union Savings Bank have yet to be built. Today's photograph shows that even in a small village, what once dominated the landscape can itself become obscured. The house next to the church is the residence of W.D. Gerard.

A 8099 M. E. Church, Patchogue, L. J.

From
Ella

Looking north on South Ocean Avenue in this c. 1910 image, the St. Francis De Sales Church is on the west side of the street at the corner of Amity Street. It was built in 1888 on the southeast corner of Conklin Avenue and East Main Street and was moved to its current site over a period of three months starting in December 1906. The pastor, Father James J. Cronin, believed the East Main Street location was too far from the center of Patchogue.

Ocean Ave., showing St. Francis de Sales R. C. Church, Patchogue.

Lower End of Ocean Avenue,   Patchogue, L. I.

This 1913 view of South Ocean Avenue shows the Patchogue Trolley on its way to the many hotels near the last stop at the foot of South Ocean Avenue. Each car had room for 25 passengers, and top speed was about 11 miles per hour. A full charge of its batteries would allow the trolley to go about 52 miles. Today's photograph has the house with the turret hidden behind the trees. The hydrant is still in the same place.

The Algonquin, 561 S. Ocean Ave.   Patchogue, L. I., N. Y.

Phone 1726   M. T. Quinn, Mgr.

This photograph of the Algonquin Hotel is from 1926 and is another one of E.E. Brown's that was published as a postcard. The building is on the northeast corner of Smith Street and South Ocean Avenue. Except for the alterations to some of the windows and the partial enclosing of the front porch, it looks very much the same now as it did then. It now serves as apartments.

The Ocean Avenue Hotel was right on the Great South Bay on the east side of South Ocean Avenue. The original section was built in 1878 under the ownership of Sanford Weeks. Later additions increased its capacity significantly, so that by the time of this photograph in 1908, it could accommodate 275 guests. Additional services included a livery stable where horses and carriages could be rented. Today, the site is part of Shore Front Park and overflow parking for Lombardi's on the Bay restaurant.

Ocean Ave. Hotel, Patchogue, L. I.

The new Mascot House Hotel was at the foot of South Ocean Avenue opposite the Ocean Avenue Hotel. Constructed in the early 1880s, it was owned by Ruth Newey Smith and operated as the Rogers House by George Rogers. It was later called the Pasco Hotel and then the Bay Side Hotel before becoming the new Mascot after the original Mascot was moved from the dock that extended out into the bay. Today, the site is occupied by Lombardi's on the Bay.

The New "Mascot", Patchogue, L. I.

CHAPTER 3

BY THE RIVERS AND THE BAY

This tranquil scene from 1913 shows the Patchogue River looking north from the railroad bridge, slightly north of Division Street. In the background are some of the buildings that comprised the Patchogue Plymouth Mills complex, or "Lace Mill," as most of the local residents referred to it. From this angle, it could have been a small farm, but the images on pages 13 and 14 prove otherwise.

On the east side of the Patchogue River south of Division Street, Bailey's Lumber Mill was one of the largest and most successful of its kind on Long Island. This 1913 image shows the mill at the height of its operations, when it was supplying the lumber and millwork for a majority of the homes built along the south shore of Long Island. Today, the site comprises a small park, bowling alley, and the Fire Island National Seashore ferry terminal.

This 1908 view of Kate Gilbert's estate, Brightwood, was taken from the west side of the Patchogue River looking east. The estate included most of the area from the river to Cedar Avenue and from Laurel Street to the Great South Bay, with the main entrance on Laurel Street. Auctioned off in 1913, the property today includes Sandspit Park and ferry terminal, Fire Island National Seashore headquarters, and many private residences.

This photograph was taken looking north from the foot of Bay Avenue around 1911. The photographer has his back to the Great South Bay, and the entrance to the Cliffton Hotel is to the right, just out of view. The attire of the people suggests that a wedding was about to start at the hotel.

Continuing a few feet to the right (east) of the photograph on the previous page, this view shows the main entrance to the hotel. Constructed in 1882 with later additions in 1892 and 1896, it had enough rooms for 300 customers and was one of the largest hotels in Suffolk County. Guest rates were from $2.50 to $4 per day, or $15 for the week.

This front view of the Cliffton Hotel shows how magnificent the building was. With all of those rooms facing the Great South Bay and a dining hall that could accommodate all of its guests at a single seating, it is easy to understand why it was an extremely popular resort destination during the first quarter of the 20th century.

Looking west with the Great South Bay just to the left, this view gives a better understanding of the 13-acre property. The grounds included a vegetable garden, manicured lawns for tennis and croquet, an archery range, and an indoor bowling alley. A beach with bathhouses and a boardwalk were also available. The great lawn is now Breeze Drive, with Grove Avenue off to the right.

This 1906 view of the Ocean Avenue Hotel was taken looking east from the foot of South Ocean Avenue. Like the Cliffton, this hotel had many rooms facing the water. Built in 1878 and operated by Sanford Weeks, additions eventually allowed for 275 guests. The site of the main entrance is the overflow parking lot for Lombardi's on the Bay.

This 1909 view shows the full extent of the Ocean Avenue Hotel after the additions and was probably taken from the Mascot dock. With no bulkhead, concern about flooding was apparently minimal. The Roe Hotel annex was just out of view to the right. Today's photograph shows a portion of Shorefront Park, where many community events are held throughout the year.

The *Curiosity* was an oyster dredge operated by Charles Mott and his Nassau Oyster Company. It was built in Patchogue in 1894 and was the first gasoline-powered dredge on the Great South Bay. This view from about 1907 shows the vessel in a canal near the foot of Rider Avenue in the vicinity of the Shorefront Park baseball field.

This 1910 view looking north from the southern end of South Ocean Avenue shows the new Mascot House Hotel on the left and the entrance to the Ocean Avenue Hotel on the right. It is an interesting photograph that visualizes the beginning of the new form of horsepower alongside the still-viable old form. Today's photograph shows Lombardi's on the Bay on the left, with the edge of Shorefront Park on the right.

Foot of Ocean Avenue, Patchogue, L. I.

This image from about 1910 was taken from the same location as the photograph on the previous page except looking south. The dock shows no evidence of its former tenant, the old Mascot House Hotel, which had been recently removed. Today's photograph has 14 streetlights instead of just one, but the view and the breeze are the same.

The Mascot House was one of the first hotels built on the bay in Patchogue. After acquiring a lease from the Town of Brookhaven, John N. Silsbe built the dock and hotel sometime in the 1880s. The building was repurposed as an oyster shed after it was moved slightly east around 1905.

Mascot Dock, Patchogue, L. I.

This view looking north shows the old Mascot House Hotel before it was moved. With its wooden-plank dock extended into the bay, it was a prime spot to tie up for the ferry boat captains waiting for passengers who would be transported to Fire Island. The Ocean Avenue Hotel and Roe Annex can also be seen to the right.

This view from around 1910 shows the Roe cottages or bungalows that were on the bay slightly east of Cedar Avenue. Owned by the same family that operated Roe's Hotel on East Main Street, these cottages were usually rented by the week during the summer season. Today's photograph shows that the cottages have been replaced by private residences.

Ruland's Bathing Pavilion was at the foot of Cedar Avenue just west of the Roe cottages. There were separate bathhouses for men and women used by both locals and tourists who were staying at facilities far from the water. The old Mascot House can be seen in the background on the right.

A Scene at the Bathing Pavilion, Patchogue, L. I.

CHAPTER 4

AROUND THE VARIOUS LAKES

This view looking southwest from the western end of Lake Street gives a different perspective of the Patchogue Lace Mill. Patchogue Lake came within a few feet of the structure. Legend has it that two workers were arguing and one was pushed out a window into the water. This part of the lake was filled in for the extension of West Avenue to Waverly Avenue in the early 1960s.

This view shows the Lace Mill about 1907 looking southeast from the west bank of Patchogue Lake. There were over 200 employees from the adjoining villages of Sayville, Blue Point, Bayport, Medford, and Bellport. The present photograph shows a small portion of the Blue Point Brewery with its replica clock tower.

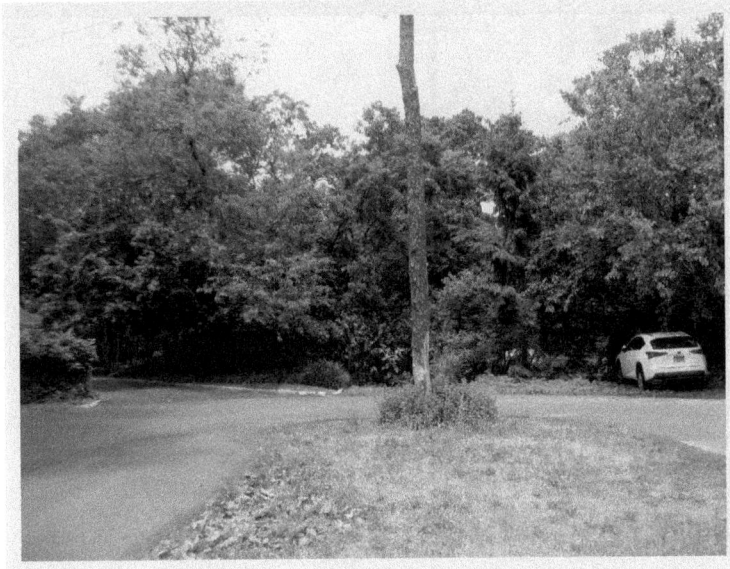

This 1907 view was taken looking north along the right-of-way of the Suffolk Traction Railway Company, which operated only from 1909 to 1919. This section is slightly northwest of Canaan Lake heading in the direction of the Holtsville Long Island Railroad station. Small segments of the right-of-way can still be found in wooded areas of Holtsville. The present photograph was taken at the north end of Traction Boulevard.

NE NEAR CANAAN LAKE,
PATCHOGUE, L. I.

266

This view of Canaan Lake is from sometime in the 1940s. It shows that the lake was a popular recreation area that rivaled the more well-known Lake Ronkonkoma and was a treasured relaxation place for area residents. There was a significant number of small cottages that were used by summer vacationers only and have since been converted into permanent residences. Today's photograph shows the exact same location. Efforts are currently underway by the Suffolk County government to restore it to its former beauty.

The Overflow, Patchogue, L. I.
Canaan Lake

This 1911 image shows water flowing out of the spillway at the southern end of Canaan Lake on its way south to Patchogue Lake and on to the Patchogue River. A culvert replaced the spillway, and the dirt path above eventually became Traction Boulevard.

This photograph is slightly earlier than the one on the previous page but was taken in approximately the same area. The two observers in the right background are probably standing near the spillway. Fishing was always good at Canaan Lake until invasive species took over, requiring the current remediation efforts.

This photograph of the Canaan lake area dates to about the same time as those on pages 69 and 70. It shows Pine Street on the right (later to become Old North Ocean Avenue) and the dirt path over the spillway to the left. This view looks north. The present photograph has all-way stop signs at the intersection and enough traffic to require a crossing guard to protect children on their way to Canaan Elementary School, a short distance to the left.

Canaan Lake
Patchogue, L. I., N. ʏ

This 1907 photograph shows the home and estate of Adm. George W. Sumner, a 45-year Navy veteran who fought in the Civil War under Adm. David Farragut. Originally built in 1887 by Clarence Vrooman, it was purchased by Admiral Sumner in 1903. The property was on the west side of Swan Lake at East Main Street. Demolished in 1943, it is now the site of a CVS store and the Suffolk Center for Rehabilitation and Nursing.

This old sawmill was one of several that dotted the landscape of Patchogue for many generations. This 1907 image shows the mill on the south side of East Main Street at Swan Lake. Judging by appearances, it had been abandoned for many years at that time. Once the site of a car dealership, it has been restored to a passive park.

Directly across East Main Street from the photograph on the previous page stood this more substantial mill. The first mill at this site was built in 1814 by Squire Mott. It burned in 1854 and was rebuilt as seen in this 1907 view. As late as 1930, it was being used as a tearoom. The mill burned in 1931, and the site was also a car dealership for many years but has been restored to open space.

Looking east along South Country Road, this 1905 image shows East Lake on the north side of the road. It was also known as Robinson Pond, because many members of the Robinson family settled in the area and still reside there today. The present photograph shows that the area still has the same rural charm with the exception of the paved road.

This view from 1911 shows the same lake as on the previous page but looking west. Just west of today's South Country Shores, water from the pond flows through Mud Creek before emptying into Patchogue Bay. As with many local ponds and lakes, invasive plant species have curtailed recreational usage.

CHAPTER

5

HERE AND THERE

The Patchogue Library was built on the south side of Lake Street just west of North Ocean Avenue on land donated by Edwin Bailey. Constructed in 1907 at a cost of $15,000 with funds donated by Andrew Carnegie, the building first opened in 1908, about the same time as this photograph. The architect was John V. Van Pelt, who also designed the post office on East Main Street. Additions were built in the 1950s, and the structure was home to Briarcliffe College for many years.

This image from 1960 shows Dodge City, a Western-themed amusement park on the southwest corner of Sunrise Highway and Waverly Avenue. Only in operation for about three years, it offered train rides and staged shoot-outs, stagecoach hold-ups, and the hanging of the bad guy. Today, the site is occupied by the Staples and King Kullen shopping center.

This 1930s photograph was taken looking east at the Mascot pool and hotel on the southwest corner of South Ocean Avenue and Maiden Lane. Most of the shorefront hotels relied on their proximity to the bay for swimming and bathing, but the Mascot offered an additional feature. The Patchogue Village Pool and Lombardi's on the Bay occupy the site today.

The Maple Avenue School was built in 1899 with four classrooms at the northwest corner of Thorne Street and Maple Avenue. Four more rooms were added in 1904. By the 1930s, construction of additional school buildings rendered this one obsolete, although it was used as an aviation training facility during World War II. Demolished in 1949, it is now the site of the Maple Tree Apartments.

Maple Avenue School, Patchogue

Construction began on this new firehouse in 1904. Located on the north side of Lake Street between Jennings Avenue and North Ocean Avenue, it replaced the first firehouse just around the corner that was opposite Oak Street. Built at a cost of $8,795 by Clarence Vrooman, it served the community well until the third firehouse was built a few yards away on Jennings Avenue in 1970.

The Lyceum, Patchogue, L. I.

The Lyceum Theatre was on the north side of Lake Street between the second firehouse and North Ocean Avenue. It was constructed in 1855 as the Congregational church but was sold in 1895, enlarged, and converted to a theater after the new Congregational church was built on East Main Street. Today, two apartment buildings and Reese's Pub occupy the site.

Shaber's Rest was a steakhouse and restaurant on the west side of Medford Avenue (Route 112) about 200 feet south of Shaber Road. As this photograph from the 1950s shows, it had the look and feel of a rural roadhouse. Today's photograph indicates that the original building has been retained and altered and is currently the Midway Motel.

The River Avenue School seemed to be in a constant state of expansion around the turn of the last century due to an ever-increasing population. This building, constructed with four classrooms in 1897 behind the original one-room schoolhouse, was enlarged to six rooms in 1906 to meet increased demand. After burning down in 1923, a new brick structure was built in 1926, with many additions since then.

P-269

RIVER AVE. SCHOO
PATCHOGUE, N. Y

This is another image of Bailey's Mill from about 1910 (see page 50). This view looks south along West Avenue to the intersection with Division Street. As the number of train tracks indicates, Patchogue was a major hub for freight and passenger rail service. Today's photograph shows only one set of tracks, with a bowling alley in the background.

Constructed in 1889, the Patchogue train station served the community for almost 75 years. In this 1910 photograph facing west, station wagons are lined up waiting to bring guests to the various hotels. In the distance are the water tower and freight house. The station building was demolished in 1963 to allow for more parking and the eventual construction of a high-level platform to accommodate more modern train cars.

This view, looking east from Railroad Avenue around 1914, includes a portion of the freight platform on the left. The freight operations, with additional tracks and sidings, are out of view behind the photographer. Today's image, taken from West Avenue, shows that Railroad Avenue has been eliminated south of the tracks along with the freight buildings.

The first high school was built in 1871 and was also known as the academy. It was on the east side of South Ocean Avenue between the railroad tracks and Academy Street. The school was designed with two large classrooms on each floor; they each were subsequently divided in half, and a two-story addition was built to the rear.

The High School,
Patchogue, L. I.

With the construction of a new high school on South Ocean Avenue in 1923–1924, the academy eventually became surplus. It was repurposed, however, by moving half of it about 1,000 feet east on Academy Street and turning it 90 degrees clockwise. It now serves as the home of Serene Home Nursing Agency. The Civil War memorial was moved to the American Legion building on South Ocean Avenue.

This photograph of Wilmott M. Smith Grammar School was taken at about the same time as the first classes in 1908. It is probable that the first principal, Frederick Vanderwater, is pictured along with his teaching staff. Located on Bay Avenue, it was the first all-brick school building in Patchogue. In 1964, Bay Avenue School was built directly in front of it, and the old building was demolished.

The Palm Pines Restaurant was at 347 Grove Avenue, according to the information on the back of this c. 1920 image. It apparently was not in operation very long, since no other information can be located about the establishment. It was the private residence of Dr. Charles F. Walter in 1926 and today is still a residence, although with several alterations.

The Winona Hotel was at 380 Bay Avenue and was built around 1880. A medium-sized hotel, it had accommodations for up to 75 guests. Although the top two floors were severely damaged by fire, it was repaired and continued as the Halcyon Manor, a home for the elderly. Today, it has been completely refurbished into the headquarters for the Patchogue Village Parks Department.

This 1907 photograph shows Tower House at 333 Rider Avenue. It was a seasonal boardinghouse operated by Charles A. Miller during the first quarter of the 20th century. Unlike a hotel, it only offered rooms and meals during the summer, with no other amenities. The present photograph shows it as a private residence minus the tower.

This image from around 1930 shows the fountain on the Avery property in East Patchogue. The Swan River Nursery was started in the 1890s by Humphrey Avery on land that had been in his family since the early 1700s. The fountain was built to attract customers when Montauk Highway was extended through his property. The present photograph shows that the fountain still exists, although reclamation by nature makes finding it difficult.

This is a current view of the Carnegie Library building shown on page 77. It was moved from its former location on Lake Street to the corner of West Avenue and West Main Street and restored. Through the combined efforts of the Patchogue-Medford Library District, Tritec Real Estate, the Knapp-Swezey Foundation, the Incorporated Village of Patchogue, Suffolk County, and the Friends of the Carnegie Library, it is now home to the Patchogue-Medford Library's teen center and the Greater Patchogue Historical Society.

Visit us at
arcadiapublishing.com